to my brother,

By Eden Willow

introduction

this book is a tribute to you, my brother.

my steadfast supporter, my lifelong ally, my remarkable brother.

you are the keeper of shared memories, the companion of the present, and a constant in all my tomorrows.

words fall short to express my affection for you, so for the next 100 days, let each morning bring you a sprinkle of joy.

every page holds a daily affirmation, a boost of positivity, and a subtle reminder of your inner resilience.

you are truly exceptional, and i hope you never lose sight of the extraordinary person you are.

you hold a special place in my heart.

with deepest affection,

to my brother

DAY #*1*

remember those endless summer days we spent exploring, laughing, and dreaming under the sun?

those memories are my treasures, reminders of the bond we share.

to my brother

DAY #2

seek wisdom not just in success but in silence, in nature, in the stories of those who came before us.

listen to the world around you, for it has much to teach.

to my brother

DAY #3

do you recall those nights we stayed up late, talking about everything and nothing?

those conversations shaped me more than you know.

i cherish every word, every shared silence.

DAY #4

your journey, marked by persistence and grace, is a story of true resilience.

i am so proud of everything you've overcome and all that you are.

to my brother

DAY #5

in you, i find a mirror of my own soul.

our shared experiences, our shared lineage, our shared dreams.

thank you for being an irreplaceable part of my life, my brother, my ally, my twin spirit.

DAY #6

watching you overcome every hurdle with such grace and determination fills me with immense pride.

you handle life's challenges with a strength that inspires me every day.

to my brother

DAY #7

as we journey through life, i see endless possibilities unfolding
before us.

together, we can conquer the highest peaks and explore the
deepest valleys.

our shared dreams are the wings that will take us there.

DAY #8

you have a way of making everyone feel special, seen, and heard.

your kindness is a rare gift in this world.

thank you for spreading light wherever you go, and especially into my life.

to my brother

DAY #9

you've always been more than just a brother; you're a true friend, a confidant.

i'm here for you, to listen, to understand, to walk with you through every storm.

to my brother

DAY #*10*

in every success of yours, i find a reason to celebrate.

your accomplishments are a testament to your hard work and dedication, and i couldn't be prouder.

to my brother

DAY #11

keep your dreams alive and chase them with vigor, but remember to pause and appreciate the journey.

the beauty of life often lies in the journey, not just the destination.

14

to my brother

DAY *#12*

remember, i'm just a call away whenever you need to talk or just sit in silence.

your feelings are valid, and i'm here to understand and support you, no matter what.

to my brother

DAY *#13*

in the tapestry of the future, i see us weaving our dreams into
reality.

side by side, we'll turn aspirations into achievements, hopes
into happenings.

to my brother

DAY *#14*

the sound of your laughter echoing through our childhood
home, the games we played, the secrets we shared - these
moments are etched in my heart forever.

DAY #15

our shared history is a treasure trove of joy, laughter, and learning.

every memory with you is a reminder of the unspoken, enduring love of siblings.

to my brother

DAY #*16*

it's a miracle we survived our childhood adventures.

between our bike stunts and tree climbing escapades, we really should have had our own reality show.

to my brother

DAY #*17*

i never told you, but i always let you win at arm wrestling.

okay, that's a lie, but let's pretend, for the sake of my ego

to my brother

DAY *#18*

you've been my confidant, my ally, my guide - in you, i find an unconditional love that strengthens me, that fills my life with warmth and light.

to my brother

DAY #*19*

our journey together is a testament to the enduring power of
love.

in every shared smile, every shared tear, i find the depth of my
affection for you.

to my brother

DAY #*20*

you've always had this incredible way of making the ordinary feel extraordinary.

with you, even the smallest moments turn into cherished memories.

thank you for filling my life with such magic.

to my brother

DAY #*21*

don't fear failure; it's merely a stepping stone on the path to success.

every setback teaches a lesson, every obstacle presents an opportunity to grow.

to my brother

DAY #22

through laughter and tears, triumphs and trials, the love we share remains unshaken.

it's a bond forged in affection, strengthened by time, and deepened by understanding.

to my brother

DAY *#23*

thanks for all the fashion advice over the years.

without you, i'd probably still be wearing socks with sandals.

to my brother

DAY *#24*

you have a way of facing challenges head-on, never losing sight of who you are.

your resilience is not just inspiring, it's a lesson in character and strength.

to my brother

DAY *#25*

we've laughed together, cried together, and grown together.

our bond is unbreakable, our connection eternal.

thank you for being not just my brother, but my best friend.

to my brother

DAY *#26*

remember, no matter how tough the road gets, you're not walking it alone.

i'm here, right beside you, every step of the way.

your strength is my strength.

to my brother

DAY #27

in you, i see a future filled with brilliance and adventure.

let's keep inspiring each other to reach for the extraordinary.

to my brother

DAY #*28*

your wisdom and insight have guided me through life's twists and turns.

you always seem to know just what to say, just when i need to hear it.

thank you for being my mentor and my confidant.

DAY *#29*

looking back at all we've shared fills me with such warmth and nostalgia.

we've grown and changed, but our memories remain timeless, eternal.

to my brother

DAY #*30*

your laughter has been my greatest comfort, your words my guiding light.

in the darkest of times, it was you who showed me how to find the stars.

thank you for being my constant in a world of change.

to my brother

DAY #*31*

the way you see the world, full of wonder and possibility, has always inspired me.

you turn the mundane into magic, the ordinary into extraordinary.

thank you for sharing your unique perspective with me.

to my brother

DAY *#32*

life will throw curveballs, but remember, it's not about avoiding them, it's about learning to catch.

embrace the unexpected, for it often leads to beautiful destinations.

to my brother

DAY #*33*

your kindness, your laughter, your unwavering support - these
are the threads that weave the tapestry of my love for you, a
tapestry rich and deep.

to my brother

DAY #*34*

the laughter, the tears, the triumphs, and the trials - every
moment with you is a cherished memory, a precious piece of
the tapestry of my life.

to my brother

DAY #35

life's richest lessons often come from unexpected sources.

remain open, curious, and willing to learn from every person
and every experience.

DAY #*36*

life has thrown its curveballs, but you've faced them with an
unbreakable spirit.

remember, i'm here to share your burdens and celebrate your
victories, always.

to my brother

DAY #37

in you, i've found a safe harbour in life's storms.

your strength is my shelter, your laughter my relief.

together, we're unstoppable.

to my brother

DAY #*38*

those childhood games, the inside jokes only we understand,
the way we could communicate without words - such memories
are the foundation of our unbreakable bond.

to my brother

DAY #*39*

your ability to find light in the darkest of times is something i
admire deeply.

know that i'm here to share both your joys and your sorrows,
every step of the way.

to my brother

DAY *#40*

may the coming years be filled with adventures we've yet to dream of.

i look forward to every laugh, every challenge, and every triumph we'll share.

to my brother

DAY #*41*

i've seen you face challenges with such dignity, and i want you to know, i'm always here to lend an ear or a shoulder.

your journey is as important to me as my own.

to my brother

DAY *#42*

for every time you listened, every hug you gave, every moment you spent just being there for me.

these simple acts mean more than you can imagine.

thank you for your unwavering support and love.

to my brother

DAY #43

let's promise to always chase our dreams, no matter how far or how hard.

with you by my side, i believe we can achieve anything we imagine.

to my brother

DAY *#44*

i admire your strength and resilience.

know that i'm here, not just as your sibling, but as someone who truly understands and supports you.

to my brother

DAY *#45*

in moments of doubt, remember that you're backed by an
unwavering support system.

i'm here for you, believing in you, even on the days you might
not believe in yourself.

to my brother

DAY #46

our past is just the beginning of a story yet to be written.

let's fill the next chapters with aspirations turned into reality, side by side, as only brothers can.

to my brother

DAY *#47*

your courage in the face of adversity is a lesson in strength.

you've taught me that being brave isn't about never being scared, it's about facing fears head-on.

you are my role model in bravery.

to my brother

DAY *#48*

here's to all the times we laughed so hard we couldn't breathe.

i'm pretty sure we've invented a new form of abs workout.

to my brother

DAY *#49*

in every challenge, you've shown such strength, and i want you to know i'm here for you, always.

your courage in the face of adversity is not just inspiring, it's a lesson in resilience and grace.

to my brother

DAY *#50*

when the going gets tough, remember that you're tougher.

you've proven it time and again.

i believe in you, always and in all ways.

to my brother

DAY #51

watching you navigate life with such passion and purpose is
awe-inspiring.

you've shown me that with hard work and determination,
anything is possible.

i am endlessly inspired by your zest for life.

to my brother

DAY #*52*

every step you've taken, every goal you've achieved, has filled me with such pride.

you're not just my brother; you're a role model who constantly inspires me to be better.

DAY #53

in every challenge you face, know that you have an endless well of courage within you.

i've seen you conquer so much already.

keep going, you've got this.

to my brother

DAY *#54*

here's to a future where we continue to lift each other higher, chase our wildest dreams, and make the impossible possible.

together, there's nothing we can't achieve.

to my brother

DAY #55

our shared adventures, big and small, are the chapters of a story
only we know.

each memory a brushstroke in the beautiful painting of our
siblinghood.

DAY *#56*

the love i feel for you is a constant source of comfort and strength.

it's a love that transcends time and distance, a bond that is unbreakable, eternal.

to my brother

DAY #57

recall our secret handshake that we thought was so cool?

i still do it sometimes when meeting new people.

it's a great way to weed out the boring ones.

to my brother

DAY #*58*

you're not just a brother; you're a piece of my heart, a fragment of my soul.

the love i have for you is as vast as the ocean, as endless as the sky.

to my brother

DAY #59

i still can't believe you convinced me that the ice cream truck
only played music when it was out of ice cream.

i owe you for years of missed treats – prepare for a lifetime of
pranks in return.

to my brother

DAY *#60*

through all of life's twists and turns, you've been my steady.

when i was lost, you were my guiding light.

your wisdom and love have shaped who i am.

to my brother

DAY #61

i dream of a future where we continue to grow, learn, and explore this vast world together.

our shared aspirations are the roadmap to an incredible journey.

to my brother

DAY *#62*

growing up with you has been the adventure of a lifetime.

from scraped knees to shared dreams, every moment with you
is a treasure.

here's to a lifetime more of adventures.

to my brother

DAY #63

i often find myself smiling at random memories of us - our silly antics, our quiet moments, our shared discoveries.

these memories are my comfort, my joy.

to my brother

DAY *#64*

my world is brighter, kinder, and infinitely richer because you're in it.

your presence is a gift i cherish every day, a source of endless love and joy.

to my brother

DAY #*65*

in moments of doubt, trust your instincts.

they are the whispers of wisdom passed down through our
shared experiences and the lessons we've learned together.

to my brother

DAY *#66*

in your pursuit of greatness, don't forget to nurture your inner peace.

it's from a place of calm that the clearest decisions are made.

to my brother

DAY *#67*

balance ambition with humility, confidence with compassion.

the true measure of success is not just what you achieve, but how you uplift others along the way.

to my brother

DAY #68

as we've grown, i've watched you turn trials into triumphs.

your resilience and grace under pressure inspire me every day.

thank you for being my personal hero.

to my brother

DAY *#69*

seeing you chase your dreams with such passion and
commitment fills my heart with pride.

your enthusiasm and determination are contagious.

DAY #70

the future is a canvas, and i can't wait to paint it with you.

every color will tell a story of our dreams, our hopes, and the journey we share.

to my brother

DAY #71

do you remember when we were kids and played superhero?

i've come to realize you don't need a cape to be my hero.

but it wouldn't hurt to wear one now and then for old times' sake.

to my brother

DAY #72

you taught me to be brave, to stand up for myself, to chase my
dreams with relentless passion.

your example has shaped the person i am today.

thank you for being my role model and my friend.

to my brother

DAY #73

i carry a part of you wherever i go, a reminder of the love and warmth you've always given me.

our bond is a rare treasure, a beacon of true brotherly love.

to my brother

DAY #*74*

remember when we tried cooking dinner for mom and dad and nearly set the kitchen on fire?

who knew that smoke alarms could be such effective dinner bells?

to my brother

DAY #75

you know you're my favorite brother, right?

of course, you're also my only brother, but let's not get caught up in the details.

to my brother

DAY #76

watching you pursue your goals with such passion fills me with awe.

keep shining, keep striving, and know that i'm proud of you every day.

to my brother

DAY #77

in your moments of doubt, remember i'm here.

to listen, to empathise, to be your pillar of strength and understanding.

to my brother

DAY #*78*

life is a journey best shared with someone who understands
your soul, and that's you.

thank you for being my compass, my confidant, and my
cheerleader all rolled into one.

our bond is irreplaceable.

to my brother

DAY #79

in the tapestry of life, you're the brightest thread, adding colour
and warmth to my world.

i am forever grateful for the laughter, the tears, and the endless
support we've shared.

to my brother

DAY *#80*

your journey hasn't been easy, but the way you've navigated it with integrity and courage is truly admirable.

i'm so proud to call you my brother.

to my brother

DAY *#81*

your journey may be filled with twists and turns, but i have no doubt you'll navigate it brilliantly.

you have the talent, the will, and the heart to succeed.

to my brother

DAY *#82*

growing up with you was an adventure of a lifetime.

the memories we made, the secrets we shared, the dreams we dared to dream together.

thank you for being more than just a brother; you're a piece of my heart.

to my brother

DAY #83

let kindness be your compass and empathy your map.

in a world where you can be anything, always choose to be
understanding and compassionate.

to my brother

DAY #84

your journey, with its ups and downs, has shaped you into the
incredible person you are today.

i'm here, not just to celebrate your successes but to offer
comfort and understanding in your times of need.

to my brother

DAY *#85*

i've watched you grow and overcome so much, and it's a
privilege to be by your side through it all.

your journey is a testament to your strength, and i'm here,
always ready to listen and support you.

to my brother

DAY *#86*

your achievements are not just a reflection of your hard work
but also your incredible character.

i admire your perseverance and the way you always stay true to
yourself.

to my brother

DAY #87

through every high and every low, i'll be here, your steadfast supporter.

you've accomplished so much already, and the best is yet to come.

keep soaring, brother.

DAY *#88*

in this big, wide world, it's your heart that feels like home to me.

the love we share as brothers is my anchor, my constant, my guiding light.

to my brother

DAY #89

remember, our shared memories are more than just past times; they are lessons wrapped in love.

draw from them, and you'll find strength and wisdom for your journey ahead.

to my brother

DAY #90

in the quiet moments, i often find myself grateful for you, for the love that binds us.

it's a feeling too immense for words, a bond too profound for explanation.

to my brother

DAY *#91*

as you reach for the stars, know that i'm right here, reaching with you.

together, there's no dream too distant, no goal too great.

to my brother

DAY *#92*

in every challenge i faced, i found you right there beside me.

your strength became my strength, your courage my guide.

thank you for being my rock when i needed it most.

to my brother

DAY #93

you're capable of achieving anything you set your mind to.

i've seen your dedication and hard work.

don't stop now; greatness is just around the corner.

to my brother

DAY #94

your resilience is a beacon of hope and inspiration.

keep pushing forward; your efforts are not going unnoticed.

you're doing amazing.

to my brother

DAY #95

your dreams are worth chasing, and i'll be cheering for you at
every milestone.

don't ever doubt your abilities; you're capable of incredible
things.

to my brother

DAY *#96*

remember those long talks under the stars where we'd plan our futures?

every dream you've chased, every goal you've achieved, i've felt like i was right there with you.

your success is my joy.

to my brother

DAY #97

the resilience you've shown in the face of adversity is nothing short of remarkable.

your ability to stay positive and keep moving forward is something i deeply respect.

to my brother

DAY #98

the way you stand up for what you believe in, never wavering in your values, is something i greatly admire.

your strength of character is a beacon for me.

to my brother

DAY *#99*

from scraped knees to shared dreams, our journey together has
been the most beautiful part of my life.

i wouldn't trade those memories for the world.

to my brother

DAY *#100*

i'm still waiting for the day you'll beat me at our video game
marathons.

don't worry, i'll make sure to act surprised when it happens – in
the next century.